ALL THINGS WANT TO FLY.

———————

—R. M. Rilke

Photo credits: p. 85, Kathy Corrigan Zentgraf;
            pp. 86, 87, 88, Kelly Corrigan

Library of Congress Cataloging-in-Publication Data

Corrigan, Kelly
    Lift / Kelly Corrigan.
        p. cm.
    ISBN 978-1-4013-4124-4
1. Life. 2. Inspiration. I. Title.
    BD431.C6838 2010
    170'.44--dc22   2009044847

Book design by Shubhani Sarkar

FIRST EDITION

RRD-C
10   9   8   7   6   5   4   3

Kelly Corrigan

LIFT

voice

Hyperion   New York

L I F T

Dear Georgia and Claire,

You're both in bed now. Dad, too. I should be sleeping but I'm wound up.

First day of school's tomorrow. Bus comes at 7:44 and won't drop you off until after three. We don't usually get downstairs before nine. But tonight, shoes are by the front door and backpacks are zipped. You even laid out your clothes, so we don't have to argue in the morning.

I don't think you'll remember tomorrow, or many of the other days we've spent together so far. I only know a handful of stories from before middle school. There was the kiss by the coats in the spring of fifth grade that I pretended was gross.

And the time my teacher, who was tall but wore purple heels anyway, asked if anyone knew how to spell *chaos* and I wanted to raise my hand so badly and be the one who knew something no one else in my class knew but I couldn't because I didn't know. I feel that way still, like I wish I knew more, like I wish I had answers.

And I remember in third grade, I pulled a tiny foil star off Julia Burr's row and put it on mine, so I'd have more. I got caught and was taken to see the principal, who had very short hair that looked burnt on the ends. When she started in on me, Mrs. Ford, my teacher, held out her hand and guided me into her lap. I put part of her long necklace in my mouth—I was very nervous—and she gently took it out so I could concentrate on the principal's thoughts about truthfulness. You guys love that story.

You're always asking me to tell you about making mistakes or getting grounded. Like when I was ten and I tried to get a bug off my dad's windshield by kicking it, over and over, from the inside, until the glass cracked from top to bottom and side to side. Greenie came back to the car after paying for gas, sliding his billfold into his back pocket, and said, "Lovey! What the—?" We drove home in silence, Greenie shaking his head like he'd never met a kid with less sense. Those stories are as clear as stains compared to the everyday stuff like eating ice cream or playing Go Fish or swimming with my mom in Squam Lake, which I've seen a picture of but can't actually call up inside me. I can't feel the water, or my mom's shoulders under my hands, or her neck under my chin, I can't remember how safe and good it must have felt to ride around on her like that.

I heard once that the average person barely knows ten stories from childhood and those are based more on photographs and retellings than memory. So even with all the videos we take, the two boxes of snapshots under my desk, and the 1,276 photos in folders on the computer, you'll be lucky to end up with a dozen stories. You won't remember how it started with us, the things that I know about you that you don't even know about yourselves. We won't come back here.

You'll remember middle school and high school, but you'll have changed by then. You changing will make me change. That means you won't ever know me as I am right now—the mother I am tonight and tomorrow, the mother I've been for the last eight years, every bath and book and birthday party, gone. It won't hit you that you're missing this chapter of our story until you see me push your child on a swing or untangle his jump rope or wave a bee away from his head and think, *Is this what she was like with me?*

The last time we went to Philly to see your grandparents, Jammy taught you how to play dominos while I checked my e-mail. I listened as she explained the rules in stages, showing you all the ways to score until she was sure you understood. When you bagged your first point, she helped you move your peg up the board, winking and clicking her tongue and saying jokey stuff like *By Georgia, I think you've got it.*

When I was little, I don't think she winked or clicked or punned.

And my coming-of-age? Imagine one long string of cursing, crying, and lying followed by stomping and slamming, punctuated by the occasional kindness—*These eggs are good* or *Is your knee feeling better?* Jammy must've cut those moments into tiny pieces and rationed them to herself; for all she knew, it'd be a month until I fed her another morsel of affection.

I don't know when you'll read this. Maybe when you're a teenager? No, probably later, when you're on the verge of parenthood and it occurs to you for the first time that someone has been loving you for that long. Maybe (let's hope not) you'll read it because something's happened to one of us—my cancer came back or Dad was reading a text going across the Bay Bridge and cars collided—and you want to piece together what it was like *before*. No matter when and why this comes to your hands, I want to put down on paper how things started with us.

———

I always wanted kids—more than all other things. Not very Harvard Business School of me, I know.

There are other things I want to do, big crazy things, like make a movie and build an artists' compound and fix my printer. But at night, in the years before I met your dad, when I was talking to a God I wasn't sure I really believed in, I whittled down all my requests to one: children. You.

Greenie has this huge family and I love being inside something that big. I love the noise and hugging and high-fiving and how we tell the same ten stories every time we're together and, after that, we tell the same six jokes, all of which have titles, like "Precious" and "Probably" and "The Sportcoat Joke," which Uncle Dickie delivers with a Scottish accent and a harelip for no reason anyone can give. I remember once in college climbing onstage with a band. The music was so loud. The bass line came up through the floor into my body. That's what it's like being in a room full of Corrigans.

Kathy is my favorite. She's one of Uncle

Gene's seven kids, which I think explains her self-reliance and therapist's eye for interpersonal drama. I like her because she's so totally unguarded. I've always wanted to be like Kathy, and over the years, I've tried on various parts of her: I mimic her one-sentence e-mails in all lowercase letters, I listen to John Prine and early Bonnie Raitt. I clutter my bookshelves with unframed photographs, old lunch boxes, and homemade art. She's why I cut my hair short every couple of years and wear bandanas when it's too hot to turn on a blow-dryer. I read the books she sends me and the poets she mentions. She introduced me to Rilke, who has this line about how some harmonies can only come from shrieking, and another about how when crystal shatters, it also rings. The Rilke line that's up on my bulletin board is "the knowledge of impermanence that haunts our days is their very fragrance." So many true and delicate thoughts that prose can't touch. Promise me you'll read him.

Kathy took a job teaching high school English because she loves reading and talking about books, especially the things people accidentally reveal by empathizing with one character over another or hating a story too much or crying over a certain passage. But more than reading, she loves her students—the pregnant girls, the sassy girls that call her Mizzes, the boys who look at her chest too long. I sat in on her class once at Charlottesville High and left thinking, *God, she's important.*

I remember this one Corrigan wedding—Cousin Boo's. Kathy and I were sitting by the dance floor, picking at an unclaimed piece of cake, the way you do when you've already had enough and think you might just have one more bite and then the other person joins in and then you're sweeping up the last of the icing with the backs of your forks.

Her kids, all three of them, were on the dance floor together. I guess they were in middle school, or just starting high school. Lena was doing this move where you pull one foot behind you like you're stretching your thigh after a run, and Maggie was trying to moonwalk, and Aaron, the oldest, was doing the sprinkler.

"That's all I want, Kath. Right there. Funny kids who like each other."

She leaned into me and said, "It'll come. You'll get it. Oh! Look—"

Just then, Aaron and some other guys lifted Kathy's husband, Tony, over their heads, and Tony crowd-surfed, like Jack Black in the last scene of *The School of Rock*. People went nuts—cheering or reaching for their cameras or looking around for the father of the bride to see how this was going over with him. Over all the laughing and hollering,

I could hear Aaron's voice. "Stay stiff, Dad! Like Superman!"

Dad and I were still opening wedding presents when I started to think about getting pregnant. I'd watched so many friends struggle—Tracy's seven in vitros, Mary Ann's three miscarriages, Kristi's baby born still. Dad and I were lucky, if *lucky* is a big enough word for it. Another way of putting it is that we were spared years of torment. Here's a third way of saying it: I've had cancer twice and if I had to pick one fate for you, cancer or fertility problems, I'd pick cancer.

One well-timed roll in the hay, then two weeks later: *Gasp.* I cried—though less than you probably think, less than I did the other day when we were reading about the Lorax popping out of the tree stump and the Once-ler handing over the very last Truffula seed. That about killed me. Georgia, you hate it when I cry. All my conspicuous emoting turns you off. That fed-up look you give me at teacher retirement parties or soccer games or the winter concert is partly how I know that I am only a few years away from exasperating you by the way I apply my lipstick or talk to waiters or answer the phone or drive or walk or breathe.

Anyway, Dad hugged me and made some crack about his uber-sperm and the Teutonic Knights. I held up the pregnancy test stick and said, "Should we keep this?"

"Is that gross?"

"I don't care, I'm keeping it," I said.

Then Dad suggested we go downstairs, have a Guinness, and play some darts. So we did.

Darts is the only "sport" in which I have a real chance to beat Dad. He seems to have forgiven me for not being the athlete my family background would have predicted. All those Corrigan coaches and athletic directors and all-Americans—and me, a girl who'd hear birds singing upon entering the office supplies aisle at Radnor Pharmacy. You girls can pin your fixation with file folders, hole-punchers, and three-ring binders on me. Watching you fashion a wallet out of index cards and double-sided tape, or embellish the edges of place cards with deckle-edge scissors, or swoon over a metallic, fine-tip paint pen? Talk about genetic validation.

But back to darts. I spent the first two years after college mastering bar games with a bunch of Sigma Chi's, while somewhere in downtown Little Rock, Dad worked until midnight at the analyst desk of an investment bank. Before I challenged him to a game, he'd never held a dart. He caught on. A few years later, on our honeymoon, we ended every night playing on an outdoor dartboard, usually alongside an Indian busboy named Ibrahim, who had this unforgettable hair, perfectly cut and styled, shiny and black—the moon laid down a line on it like it was a lake. The point is, as funny as it seems, darts are kind of a romantic symbol for us.

When I finally started having contractions, forty-one weeks after the Guinness, Dad said, "Stay here. I'll get the good darts. We'll play to pass the time."

"They're on the corner of the table," I called after him. "Underneath some bibs and board books."

I have the video from that day. It's not much to watch—it took seventeen hours and an IV of Pitocin to start active labor—but every so often, you can see me bend over and wince. I'll show you, assuming you're old enough to hear me say "sweet-Jesus-mother-fucker." You know the rest of the story—the three-foot umbilical cord, the Jackson Browne song that was playing about soothing a fevered brow, the stork bite on your forehead that I can still sometimes see traces of when you get really hot or terribly upset.

I saw it last week, actually, when you came downstairs with a Safeway bag filled with paperback books and said, "I have to give these away."

"What?" I asked.

"I have to find all my other books and give them away too."

"Honey, why? What's the matter?"

"Because—I don't understand them," you said, as your bottom lip quivered. "I don't understand the words. You know all the Harry Potter books I've read?"

"Yeah?"

"I don't understand *any* of them. I read them but I don't know what's happening in them."

You stood there, totally sick with the sense that you were not smart like I told you you were, and now you had to tell me, and how could I ever love a kid who didn't understand Quidditch or the Dark Arts, divination or transfiguration?

"Oh honey, no one understands Harry Potter." I held out my arms but you didn't come.

"Margaret Faust does. Even Ruby does—and she's *six* and I'm *eight*."

"Well, I don't. All I know is that I'm a Miggle."

You sighed.

"Come here. Tell me what you were reading just now that got you so upset—"

"I was reading a book that the librarian said is *perfect* for third-grade girls! So obviously, I should not even be in the third grade because I am so stupid!" Then the collapse into me, then the cry that sounds like a sewing machine at full speed.

Eventually, you went upstairs to get the book so we could read together. You opened to page one and read aloud.

"It says Pru would give her *eye-tooth*. What is an *eye-tooth*?"

You stopped at every word you didn't know— *utter, ransacked, pitch-perfect*—no longer willing to skate past all those words and idioms.

"You feel better?" I said, after we finished the first chapter.

"Yeah. Can we keep going?"

"Of course."

"And Mom, it's Muggle."

It won't always be so easy to make your stork bite disappear.

During the four-month maternity leave that became the next eight years, I made a job for myself as a photographer. It was pretty nervy, I guess, since I didn't have any training in composition or light or printing—just a one-night seminar at Elmwood Camera. But trust me when I say there's a lot you can figure out as you go. You don't always have to be Qualified or Experienced. Nobody really knows what they're doing, except maybe gene-splitters, and even they'd probably admit that there's an unteachable art to everything.

I specialized in family "candids," even though when I got to people's houses, the kids looked like they'd just come from that glossy green salon in Oz where the Cowardly Lion had his hair curled. I shot kids in the sandbox, on the swing, in the bath; making mud pies, blowing bubbles, smelling flowers; twirling, running, laughing. The trick to pleasing the client, I figured out pretty fast, was cropping out every nick, scrape, and bruise, along with the pimply parts, the second chins, and any flash of impatience or disappointment in either parent's brow. It's embarrassing, how much we want to idealize family.

Before I photographed you girls, I licked you clean like a mother cat and then sat you in a patch of open shade where the sun wouldn't make you squint or drape you with shadows. I framed out the dirty cuffs of your shirts and the neon plastic toys you wouldn't put down. I shot down on you so your eyes would seem bigger. I made you smoother and more beautiful than you could have ever been. Except you were, for a second. I was there. I saw it.

Most of the pictures taken after you turned four and became self-conscious have no character. You couldn't stand in front of a camera without making a peace sign or bunny ears or baring your teeth like you do for the dentist. The only good shots I got after that were when you were too consumed by something—weaving a hot-pot holder, peeling off your toenail polish, memorizing the dialogue between Troy and Gabriella—to notice me skulking around with my Nikon.

I had my camera the day Claire put her foot in the ocean for the first time. We'd stopped off at a stretch of beach after lunch at this greasy, delicious Mexican place and even though it was too cold to swim, Claire, you stripped off your clothes and greeted the sea like an audience, or your oldest friend. Before we got back in the car, you had to wash the sand off your body in one of those almost-painful public showers where the pressure's been set too high. You found so many ways to thrill yourself in those jet streams, ways that would make your Catholic grandmother blanch. Neither

Dad nor I were inclined to stop you. You're only two and a half once.

———

After a couple of years of family photography jobs around Berkeley, Children's Hospital in Oakland hired me to take the cover shot for its donor report. I was so flattered. I charged my batteries and packed up my macro lens— the one for super close-up shots, like eyelashes and baby toes—and drove to Oakland, thinking that I should go for one of those hand-in-hand shots, a big adult hand holding a preemie hand. I hoped the newborn's fingers would be small enough to make the contrast really dramatic. I actually *hoped* that.

I was a few minutes early, so I hung around the lobby waiting and watching. A young guy came in on a bike, wearing his baseball hat backward, looking like the boys I knew in college. I watched him dig around in his pocket and show the nurse his license, and she nodded. "Your son is in Room Eleven. I'll take you back." I started looking around at everyone then, wondering what news they were waiting to get and which of them seemed the most ready.

I drifted over toward a huge dollhouse by the check-in counter and marveled at the tiny lamps with pleated fabric shades and pulls no bigger than sesame seeds. In the parlor, there was a miniature silver tea set that had a pitcher, a spoon, and a sugar bowl with a lid that you'd need tweezers to pick up. Upstairs, a girls' room had twin spool beds with pink coverlets. The whole thing was protected by Plexiglas, to make sure nothing bad happened to it.

Eventually, I was led into the NICU, where the babies were the same way—tiny, mesmerizing, protected by Plexiglas. Ken, a small, earnest guy who escorted me around, took me to Leon, born the day before, at fourteen ounces. He had a tube down his throat and wires taped to his chest. Near his face, someone had laid a piece of fabric about as big as a gum wrapper. Ken said it was a scent square.

"Parents wear the fabric on their skin—moms tuck it in their bras, dads rub it between their fingers—and before they leave for the night, they set the square by the baby's nose," Ken said, "so he'll know them when they return."

My mouth went dry. I found an Altoid in my purse and sucked it like it was an anti-anxiety pill, or a pacifier. Ken introduced me to William, a NICU nurse who'd been singled out for his giant hands. I snapped my lens into place and positioned Leon's hand in William's. People would respond to the image of those tiny fingers, they'd write checks, even without seeing the scrawny legs, the bulging, salamander eyes, the baggy skin that had been expecting so much more.

Ken and the hospital folks loved the photographs, and in time I buried the memory of that room full of eggshell fragility and found ways to convince myself that I'd never have to go back to Children's.

When the printed brochure arrived in the mail a month later, I held it out for Dad and said, "Claire was born ten times bigger than that baby. Can you imagine?"

But Dad doesn't play that game. He'll stew all night about a technicality in a contract at work that may or may not lead to a spat with a strategic partner, but real things? Things involving you guys? I don't think he can bear to consider them, so he lowers his emotional garage door and locks it from the inside.

———

I squandered the last summer we spent in the Lew-
iston Avenue apartment, the one in Berkeley that
you can't remember. Georgia, you were almost two,
Claire, you were just a baby and, truthfully, I was
wishing you both older. Especially you, Claire. I
wanted you to sleep, just until 4 a.m., then 5, then
6. When you woke up in the night, I'd reswaddle
you in the straitjacket hold and tuck you into the
vibrating seat. For hours. I've since heard that seat
referred to as the Neglect-O-Matic. And I didn't
breast-feed you long enough. You started every
feeding with a bite that made my toes curl, and I
wanted to get pregnant again before Dad changed
his mind, and then you and I passed thrush back
and forth between your mouth and my nipples for
a month and that was it. Eleven weeks. You were

a healthy baby, ten pounds at birth. I knew you'd be fine. Even so, I felt sheepish about stopping, especially living in Berkeley, where I once saw a bilingual four-year-old lift his mother's shirt at a barbecue saying, "Mama, *leche*!" But if you have allergies or undue colds, I'm sure it's my fault and I'm sorry.

One Friday night, toward the end of the summer, Claire, you got your first fever. Dad was taking out the recycling, a Diaper Genie sausage over his shoulder like a garland, and I was doing the last of the dishes. We were both watching the clock, waiting for the babysitter to unleash us for the night. I felt your forehead. I looked at Dad like maybe we should stay home, and he said, "Yeah, all right, it'd be good to save the money anyway."

Your fever held all weekend. On Monday, little red dots like paprika turned up around your diaper area. Sarah came over after work.

Sarah was your pediatrician. We picked her because she went to Harvard (especially appealing to Dad) and worked less than a mile from our apartment (especially appealing to me). After I got to know her, I insisted—several times over many months—that she have a drink with our single friend Mike, even though Dad thought Mike would "geek it" since Sarah was "pretty good-looking." A year later, they were engaged, and we'd secured a lifetime of house calls.

Sarah checked your ears and throat. She looked at the bottom of your feet and between your toes. Then she rubbed her thumb over the string of dots. "I'm checking for blanching," she said. "See how they stay red? That's different than a rash. A rash would turn white."

"Okay . . . ," I said.

"Well." Sarah closed your diaper and handed you to me. "I don't want to panic you, Kelly, but I think you should take her over to Children's Hospital, to get some tests."

"You want me to take her to Children's Hospital?"

"Just to be on the safe side," she said, nearly convincing me.

"Um, okay, that's fine," I said to Sarah, projecting composure as best I could. "Edward should be home soon, so I can leave Georgia with him and get over there."

"Okay. Call me after you talk to him." Sarah left and I dialed Dad. Before I could tell him much of anything a call came through on the other line. It was Sarah. She had called Children's.

"Give Georgia to a neighbor. You need to get Claire in there. They're expecting you."

"Why?" I stood up, looking at Claire in her bassinet.

Sarah said the tiny red dots around your diaper

area were petechiae, which sometimes indicate meningitis.

"Oh my God," I said, in a state of animal panic. "Georgia—! Sarah, what exactly *is* meningitis?"

"An infection—in the membranes that protect the brain and the spinal cord—"

My scalp prickled. My hands were shaking. I darted around the first floor, looking for keys, my purse, the diaper bag. Georgia, you were in the kitchen taping things together like you loved to do—an egg carton from recycling, a white paper bag from the pharmacy, several leftover bra liners for nursing mothers that cost me a fortune.

"So just listen," Sarah said. "When you get there, they are going to take some blood and do a culture—and they're going to do a lumbar puncture, a spinal tap, and they will start her on IV antibiotics immediately—"

My vision blurred for a second, like I'd stood up too fast. "They're going to give Claire *a spinal tap*?"

"Yes," Sarah said.

"Georgia!" I put your shoes on the table in front of you. "We gotta go, right now—" I needed you to hurry but I didn't want to scare you, so I added "honey" at the end.

"It's gonna be okay," Sarah said. "But Kel, don't let anyone make you wait."

"Untreated," Wikipedia says, "bacterial meningitis is almost always fatal." Included in the entry is a color photograph of someone's shiny, purple infant whose limbs had to be amputated because the infection led to gangrene. I'd been worrying about you choking on a mancala bead or falling through the slats on the deck, but gangrene?

Dad left work to meet me at Children's. When he appeared in the waiting room, I wanted to throw myself at him, but something about his pace and his expression said he needed to see me managing, not dissolving. Looking up at him, I wished I knew his faces a little better. Cousin Kathy once told me it takes ten years to learn your spouse; we'd barely been married for three. I shook off any hint of a breakdown and said, "All the forms have been filled out. We've been waiting to go in for about five minutes." Kathy also told me once, "We're never ready for the things that happen. When the big stuff happens, we're always looking in the other direction."

A nurse called out, "Claire? Claire Lichty?" Dad and I stood. A nurse took us through double doors to an ER room where we could wait for the doctor. I held you, taking in the room. Every drawer was labeled: IV catheters, vinyl gloves, number 10 needles. Above the red trash can for biohazard waste was a laminated reminder that this was a Germ Free Zone! Against the wall was a blanket warmer, and overhead, a set of heaters the nurse referred to as French-fry lights, to keep the babies warm.

"Hi, I'm Leo Benjamin." The doctor looked down at the chart in his hands while I threw information at him.

"She's been running a fever since Friday, 101, then 102, now 104," I said. "She's not eating, or crying. She's really not herself in any way at all."

"Okay," he said, "we're going to give her some tests. We'll draw some blood, collect a urine sample, start her on an IV. We'll have to do what's called a lumbar puncture."

"Our pediatrician told us," I said, wanting him to move faster.

Dr. Benjamin nodded toward a drawer, and the nurse took out two pairs of sterile gloves. They both put them on, and the nurse took you from me. She helped Dr. Benjamin hold you down on the table. He spread your legs open at the knees and you screamed the scream that is given to each of us as a tool, the scream of violation. I started to lunge forward but Dad took my arm. The doctor pulled back the skin above your vagina to access your urethra and insert a catheter. I stepped closer to the table, into the heart of your vehemence, as urine drained into a clear plastic bag. It's one thing to know your child is in pain, it's another to attend it. Finally, Dr. Benjamin secured the catheter and you were back in my arms. We were both sweating.

Next, we were shown to a room just for spinal taps, where a staffer stood tall like a naval cadet. "This is Jeff. He positions and stabilizes the babies during the procedure," Dr. Benjamin explained.

Jeff held out his hands. Against every instinct, I handed you off. With your feet in one hand and your forearms in the other, Jeff rounded you out. After swabbing your back with yellow iodine, Dr. Benjamin pushed a long needle between two of your lower vertebrae, "past some dura mater." Your razory screams tormented me. I crossed my arms and bit down on my lips and rocked back and forth in a soothing motion, like I'd accidentally driven into a bad neighborhood and was assuring myself that somehow I'd find my way out. I didn't look at Dad. I couldn't spare the emotion.

Dr. Benjamin pulled the needle back slowly, calmly, despite your awful shrieking. "That's all we need. We'll take this to the lab and start the evaluation." He stood and handed you to me. You were hot and whimpering. I held you, heart to heart, your hands around my neck. Although I'd betrayed you, although I'd stood by while people spread and bent and stabbed you, you still wanted me most of all.

"We can start her on antibiotics now. Stephanie will put an IV in," Dr. Benjamin said.

Our friend Deirdre is a pediatric ER doc in

Boston. She told us this thing once, long before I became a parent, that I've never forgotten. She said no matter how stark the diagnosis, parents never fall over or scream like they do on TV. They keep breathing and listening and asking very good questions, and minute-by-minute they expand on the spot to take it in. I hoped I was that adaptive. I hoped I was as sturdy as the dad in baggy shorts with his hat flipped around.

I'd been steady and reasonable for both Dr. Benjamin and the nurse, playing to the audience as I do, but after they left, I said to Dad, "This is too— I don't know. If we get out of here okay, I'll never have another baby."

"Fine with me," he said, like maybe he regretted something.

"Yeah?"

"I don't know—let's just get through this," he said, standing over your metal crib, which looked more like a cage. He shook his head like he was just now internalizing your baby-ness. "This is the first time she's seemed small to me," he said. You tricked us by coming into the world so big and loud and strong.

He had to leave. Someone had to pick up Georgia from Shannon's house.

"Kiss me, Eddy."

Dad leaned over and kissed me. "She's gonna be okay, Kel."

That first day in Children's, you probably slept twelve hours. Every few hours, I tried to get you to take a bottle, but you didn't want it. Sister Bernice stopped by to ask if I had any questions about insurance, parking validation, anything at all. Something about a nun going room to room reminded me of old war movies. I started to say, "I just want her to wake up," but my voice was shaky so I just shook my head *no*. I didn't want her to hug me or crack me wide open and do therapy on me.

"Well, if you need me, just ask the nurses to page me," she said. "All right, dear?" I felt my face flush as I nodded, like I was back in third grade with Mrs. Ford's necklace in my mouth.

Dad came to sit. He had a report from home—someone had invited us to a black-tie party at a champagne lounge, we got a postcard from the dentist about an appointment next week, Georgia fought to wear her fleece kitty-kat jacket even though it was 75 degrees. I wanted to break in with "How can you possibly care?" but I decided not to. For all I knew, Dad was self-medicating with to-do lists and calendars. I didn't respond at all, which I knew was a rejection of sorts, a way of leaving him alone, but it was better than lashing out.

Dr. Benjamin came by to check in and assure us

they were keeping an eye on the cultures. I asked him when you would get your appetite back. He said maybe the next day, and reminded me that you were being hydrated through the IV and that was the important thing.

Early the next morning, while Dad was home with Georgia, I walked around the hospital. I found myself in the parents' lounge. There were pens and paper, a fax, a printer, and power strips, so multiple people could plug in while their kids had bone marrow transplants or slept off chemo or waited for their femurs to reset. I picked up a brochure about a summer camp—archery, sailing, crafts—for kids with cancer. I read a poster about Beads of Courage, a program where kids get a new bead for every shot and pill and procedure until, I suppose, their necklaces drape on the ground. At that point, I had no beads of courage myself. Mono, chicken pox, tonsillitis, that's what I knew of shots and hospitals.

It'd be another year before an oncology nurse settled me in for my first bag of chemotherapy.

Next door was a play space for all the kids who couldn't go outside because they couldn't risk the everyday germs that the rest of us sneeze all over each other without concern or repercussion. The shelves were crowded with wooden puzzles, coloring books, stuffed animals, some costumes. A Corn Popper Push Along was leaning against the wall, near a rocking horse. If necessary, I gathered from the bouquet of withering balloons in the corner, kids could have their birthday parties here. And I had recently announced to Dad that we *had* to take you guys to Disneyland one year for a birthday treat.

I wandered back to our room and slumped in the recliner. I was so tired, things were kind of gauzy. An infection in your membrane. How thin is a membrane? I stretched a white sheet from my shoulders to my knees, like I was on a cross-country red-eye, and then put my head back down. TO LOWER BAR, LIFT THEN SQUEEZE, that's what the plaque on your crib said. It seemed so simple, but only the nurses were able to do it without a struggle.

On day three, you sucked a bottle dry. The sound of that milk being pulled through that nipple, I can hear it now. Right after Dad showed up, Dr. Benjamin strode in beaming and announced that the culture was in and you had viral meningitis, "the good kind." Dad jumped up to shake his hand.

We thanked Dr. Benjamin as a nurse came in to unhook you. I hovered as she unwrapped the splint, pulled the tape off your hand, slipped out the needle, and put a tiny band-aid on, all in a single motion.

"She's all yours," the nurse said, as I picked you up.

The relief was physical, like cold water on a burn.

I signed forms with my free hand and cleared our things out of the room and waited with you by the exit. You held my finger and I rotated my attention from you to the driveway to the wall across from me—it was a mural, a landscape photograph that obeyed the rule of thirds, a principle of composition I'd learned in that one-night seminar at Elmwood Camera. The bottom third was the city of Oakland, the middle third was clouds, and the top third was blue sky. Someone, whoever was in charge of lobby decorations, I guess, had glued a small wire-and-mesh butterfly to the image, above the clouds. Could something that small really survive at that altitude?

Dad pulled up out front. He jumped out to open

the back door and kissed you before he snapped you into the car seat. I leaned in the other side to tuck a blanket around your chin so the straps wouldn't rub against you. We drove away, into Berkeley, past the people walking with their coffee and cell phones, their shopping bags and strollers, their backpacks and school books and skateboards.

But the smell of the hospital, the sting of those overhead lights in the night, the snippets of conversation I'd overheard stayed with me and marked the beginning of how I came to know what a bold and dangerous thing parenthood is. Risk was not an event we'd survived but the place where we now lived.

———

I've done a few daring things—scuba diving, sky-diving, bungee jumping—but after I had you guys, that kind of thing lost its appeal. There *are* parents who still chase the double-black-diamond high—rock climbing, motorcycling, white-water kayaking. My friend Tracy's husband, Tom, is into hang gliding, loves it beyond all reason. Sometimes, he's up there for four or five hours. I visited Tracy and Tom last spring on the way home from my college reunion, and over a Costco hamburger and a stiff mojito on the back deck, I battered Tom with hang-gliding questions. Don't you get tired? How do you know where you're going? If there's no motor, what keeps you up?

"Basically," he said, "you fly from thermal to thermal, looking for lift."

I loved the way that sounded—flying from thermal to thermal, looking for lift. Something about it made instant sense to me and I wanted to say, "Don't we all?" Instead I said, "What's a *thermal*?" and he explained that a thermal is a column of hot air surrounded by turbulence.

"I assume you want to avoid turbulence?"

"No," he said. "Well—some turbulence is really dangerous. I actually had a friend, Terry." Tracy stopped doing the dishes and leaned against the counter. "We were flying together and he got caught in something—a sudden patch of sink, we don't really know—but he landed too fast." Tom looked over at Tracy, who was folding a dishrag. "And he died."

"Jesus," I said. We spent a while talking about Terry, his wife, his family, that horrendous day, and then I brought it back to hang gliding. "So, why would you ever go near turbulence?"

"Turbulence is the only way to get altitude, to get lift. Without turbulence, the sky is just a big blue hole. Without turbulence, you sink."

I understood what he was saying.

"I just think," I said, "I mean, the expense

alone—then you layer onto that all the work involved. Then the danger . . ."

But you know what Tom said?

"I'm really careful and I love it. I mean, I'm *flying*."

People rarely rave about their childhoods and it's no wonder. So many mistakes are made.

I see how that happens now, how we all create future work for our kids by checking our cell phones while you are mid-story or sticking you in the basement to watch a movie because we love you but we don't really want to be with you anymore that day, or coming unhinged over all manner of spilt milk—wet towels, unflushed toilets, lost *brand-new!* whatevers.

Almost every day I yell at one of you so loudly

that my throat hurts afterward. That's why I keep lozenges in practically every drawer in the house. I hold it together and hold it together and then, when the bickering picks up again, I just detonate. Like yesterday, Claire, when I listened to you whine through two rounds of some card game called Egyptian War. Finally, it was Georgia's turn to go first, and you said you couldn't play anymore because your armpits were sore. "That's stupid," Georgia said, and you cried, "Stupid is a mean word!" and smacked Georgia with your open palm as I watched. "GO TO YOUR ROOM RIGHT NOW, MISSY!" I hollered. "It was an accident; I fell into her on accident!" You both froze and I got to my feet and I leaned down into your faces and ranted at you through set teeth, like the heartless tyrannical caretakers in movies about orphans. I was so disgusted with both of you, your impatient overreactions, your loss of self-control— then I turned right around and disgusted myself.

If John Lennon was right that life is what happens when you're making other plans, parenthood is what happens when everything is flipped
over and spilling everywhere and you can't find a
towel or a sponge or your "inside" voice. But if my
temper has made you hesitant or tentative, is there
any atoning for that?

In a parent-teacher conference last year, Ms.
Tunney said, with obvious hesitation, "Sometimes—
sometimes, your daughter has a bit of an edge,
a way of snapping that makes the other kids pull
back." I cried when I left the classroom. I knew.

There are other mistakes, less obvious. I don't
mirror your emotions enough, though I can't
say why because when I do, it seems to calm you
down. I forget to praise your effort instead of your
achievement, I discipline by carrot and stick instead of reason, and I ignore the indisputable re-
search about the benefits of family dinner. I'm a

zero when it comes to the culinary arts—everything tastes like ground shoelaces, except my salads, which you are years away from appreciating. Until then, we go over to Beth's house and trade wine for dinner. It's a brilliant solution but sometimes, on the way home, when you go on and on about how Beth is *such a good cook* and then Dad adds his accolades about Beth's homemade red sauce and roasted broccolini and how you ate *every bite*, my mom-ego twitches and cramps, and by the time we get home I'm practically convulsing with animus.

I used to be "pretty chill," as I once heard Dad say to his friend Graham when I turned down a Corona at a two-year-old's birthday party. For instance, before I was your mom, I didn't have one of those plastic dividers for my silverware. I'd just take the basket out of the dishwasher and dump all the knives, forks, and spoons right into the drawer. My friends Mike and Andy, who coached me through the last of my single years, still talk about it. I went around the world without a credit card or a cell phone or a plan of any sort, I hitch-hiked a thousand miles, I went to Dead shows with people whose last names I didn't know, I wore green Birkenstocks to the office. I thought I'd be cooler as a mom. But then I leaned back on the delivery table and Dr. Laura Statchel pulled out a baby, and somewhere between the precious bundle that was Georgia and the placenta, all that *it's cool, no worries, sure why not?* stuff came out too.

My default answer to everything is *no*. As soon as I hear the inflection of inquiry in your voice, the word *no* forms in my mind, sometimes accompanied by a reason, often not. Can I open the mail? No. Can I wear your necklace? No. When is dinner? No. What you probably wouldn't believe is how much I want to say *yes*. Yes, you can take two dozen books home from the library. Yes, you can eat the whole roll of SweeTarts. Yes, you can camp out on the deck. But the books will get lost, and SweeTarts will eventually make your tongue bleed, and if you sleep on the deck, the neighborhood raccoons will nibble on you. I often wish I could come back to life as your uncle, so I could give you more. But when you're the mom, your whole life is holding the rope against these wily secret agents who never, ever stop trying to get you to drop your end.

This tug-of-war often obscures what's also happening between us. I am your mother, the first mile of your road. Me and all my obvious and hidden limitations. That means that in addition to possibly wrecking you, I have the chance to give to you what was given to me: a decent childhood, more good memories than bad, some values, a sense of a tribe, a run at happiness. You can't imagine how seriously I take that—even as I fail you. Mothering you is the first thing of consequence that I have ever done.

———

Every now and then there are victories, which is to say, moments when I let go, when I set aside all instruction and we dance. I remember the first time Dad played Van Halen for you. He'd just gotten home from work—it was a Friday so he was in an extra good mood—and we were goofing around in the living room, and he said, "Wait! I just thought of something," and a moment later, "Panama" started. Georgia, you were on the coffee table and about halfway through the song, you said to Dad, with the signature earnestness of a three-year-old, "I could listen to this *all day*." He tells this story a lot; I think it validates something for him, like you two have something crucial in common—or just a tacit, gut-level esteem for '80s arena rock. He turned the volume way up and when the song said *jump*, we jumped. You girls couldn't believe how rowdy we were being, and I thought, *They'll remember this—someday they'll be lying around a dorm room drinking Miller Lite and picking pepperonis off a cold pizza and say, "Our family used to have dance parties and my dad would play the music so loud we couldn't hear each other talk . . ."*

Sometimes when we're doing errands, a song'll pop into my head, and I have to write it on my hand to remember to play it for you when we get home—like that song from *Rent* about all the moments in a year and what we should be doing with them. I can't tell if you're responding to the music or to what the music is doing to me, but you always seem hooked. The kicker is when you start singing back—just hearing you say, "Five hundred twenty-five thousand six hundred minutes" is enough to trigger a little rush of Mother's High.

We've just begun talking about bigger things. The Beatles came up recently and I showed you a video of John Lennon playing "Imagine." I tried to explain why anyone would write a song about living in peace and why other people would call that person a dreamer and how sometimes people get shot for no good reason. You said, "How come they let people get guns?" and I said, "Exactly."

When Obama won, Dad and I ran home from the neighborhood party and woke you up and took you downstairs to watch the speech at Grant Park, and I had to explain why so many people were crying and shaking their heads and saying they never thought a black man would be president even though you guys kept saying, "He's brown." The day after the election, some moms were talking in the school-yard about how California banned gay marriage and you asked me if that meant our friend Joann was divorced now and all the moms jumped in to say no, and I added, "Someday, that'll be fixed," and I was mad at myself for not doing more to stop that from happening. I often feel like I'm not explaining things right to you, probably because half the time I don't understand them myself. How can I explain why someone would weep because the new president is brown or protest because a woman married the woman she loved?

Dad and I talk over each other to tell you stories about teamwork or ingenuity or resolve—Venus and Serena Williams playing each other at Wimbledon, the anonymous men who made the Golden Gate Bridge and St. Patrick's Cathedral and the Hoover Dam, Lewis and Clark and Sacajawea. I remember driving home one night under a full moon. You guys were in the way back arguing about which was larger, the sun or the moon, and after that was settled, Dad told you about Buzz Aldrin and Neil Armstrong. "They were all the way up there," I said, tapping on the car window, hardly able to believe it, as proud as I would've been if I'd managed the mission myself. "They walked on *that moon right there*."

Some of your questions have gone unanswered, or rather, too answered. When you asked why we only go to church when we're with Greenie and Jammy, I must've started and stopped six times. As I stammered on about world religion and the gods people worship, Georgia, you wiggled out of bed, strapped on a pair of my high heels, and limped over to see yourself in the full-length mirror. Claire followed you, saying, "My turn, now it's my turn!"

That night, I asked Dad if he considered himself a spiritual person and he surprised me by saying yes unequivocally.

"Really?" I said.

"You know when I feel spiritual?" he said. His

lips got all puffy, which for him is like falling to his knees and weeping. "When I'm with the girls."

We were quiet after that, but I reached over and found his hand under the comforter and squeezed it. So much of our intuition and apprehension and belief about the world turns out to be impossible to communicate, but he had told me something big, something defining.

You are sacred to me too.

———

We wanted more kids. Well, I did and Dad was willing. But after my first year of breast cancer treatment, something popped up on my left ovary. It did not wax and wane, as cysts do. It just sat there. Then it started getting bigger, and Dad was adamant that my ovaries come out, regardless of the consequences.

It was a simple procedure that left me with four

tiny scars. And it was the worst thing that ever happened to me. All those periods and backaches and Midol, and then it was over, the most essential components of my reproductive system whisked away in a bio-waste bag.

A couple months later, we packed up all the baby stuff for our friend Teresa. The BabyBjörn, a handful of binkie leashes we'd clip to your onesies, the ladybug infant nail-clippers.

"You might as well take these too," I said, handing her two mobiles. Teresa was so grateful as Dad carried the collapsed crib out to her car.

"Now we can turn that room into an office," he said, as Teresa drove away with your infanthoods in her trunk.

"Great," I said. "So we can stop raising babies and get back to work."

Dad hugged me. Georgia, you saw me crying and said, "Mommy, don't be a Weird-o."

I can't say yet how sudden menopause changed me, us. I looked at you differently, I know that. You became more and bigger. But the thing that utterly altered the way I look at you was not the cancer or the hysterectomy. It was Aaron, Cousin Kathy's lanky, broad-shouldered boy.

———

It was raining that night. A lazy summer rain. Kathy wanted Aaron to stay home but he said, "I'm just gonna swing by and say hello to some people, Momma." Years later, I asked her if he kissed her good-bye and she said, "Aaron wasn't a kisser, he was a big eye-contact guy. He had this killer gaze, so we just cut our eyes at each other and he left."

Kathy washed some dishes, changed into pajamas, met Tony and the girls downstairs for a movie, and went to bed.

It was hard to sleep—teenagers. But you can't

expect them to play Scrabble every Friday and Saturday night.

Around 3 a.m., the phone rang. It was a friend of Aaron's. A car, a convertible, had flipped.

In the pictures in the newspaper the next day, huge white sheets were draped over the car doors, to hide the ruin, but on the passenger side, I swear you could see a hand, in a loose fist, knuckles on the pavement. The police estimated the vehicle skidded sixty feet before it stopped. EMTs inflated an industrial balloon to raise the car and free the boys' bodies.

The officers stood on Kathy's stoop. She doesn't remember how the conversation went but the words were said—the combination of *your child* and *I'm sorry* and *nothing we can do* and then someone said *dead* just to make sure there was no room for misunderstanding or denial or resistance, which could easily happen because next they explained that they were taking her boy to the hospital, a place of healing.

She wanted to go with them. The officer kept telling her it wasn't necessary. Of course it was. Mothers go to the hospital with their children. We hold their hands and look at them with our most reassuring expressions and whisper encouraging things like *The medicine will help you sleep.* We slip into the hall for a minute to talk openly with doctors. We make decisions and sign forms and go back into the room wearing that same put-on look of composure. We check for signs of pain, we reposition pillows and lower the bed and curse the paper-thin shades as we darken the room the best we can. We sit, we stand, we stare and stretch, we shudder and sit back down and hold our heads and decide it's better standing. We lean over the bedside and run the backs of our fingers across our child's cheek and close our eyes in a moment of passion and physical memory of every other time we've touched that cheek, that singular orchid of a face.

The next night, Kathy took a shower, put on some Carmex, a long-sleeved T-shirt, a pair of nondescript black pants, and her most supportive shoes. Aaron's body had been released from the hospital. He was laid out at the funeral home and visitors were welcome starting at 8 p.m. Kathy said they all went—Tony, the girls, grandparents, even a few friends.

The mortician had tucked a large white blanket around Aaron, like you would a baby, so all that showed was his face, no makeup and somehow no scratches. Around Aaron's neck was a tiny cross that had once belonged to Kathy's Italian grandfather. It was thick and old-fashioned and Aaron loved it. Around his head was a wrap to cover the skull damage, almost like a white bandana. Everyone told Aaron Stories, and one by one, everyone touched him. Even Kathy. Did she want to wake him, to beg him to open his eyes and sit up and come home? Did she want to yell at him, *Be careful! The roads are slick! Drive slowly around that bend!* No, she told me later, she wanted to memorize him. They only left because a staff person came in to say that the family of the other boy—Aaron's friend Ross, who was also laid out there—were on their way over.

I tell you about Aaron because he died when you were both in diapers and his death has changed every day of our life together. I tell you about Aaron because I want you to live longer than he did. Even though I hope you have Aaron's general trust in people and his belief that things usually work out, even though I want you to love people as easily and overtly as he did, I want you to be more cautious and less optimistic. I want to keep you in the world where I can find you.

I hurt you once, Georgia. When you were three. I'd taken you to the Lawrence Hall of Science to look at displays about gravity and Saturn's rings and the crust of the earth. Afterward, we headed home for your nap. You were a great napper. On the way back to the car, you took a few steps away from me, right into traffic. I yanked you back as a car veered away from us, the driver pounding the horn. I squatted down and shook you, screaming, "Never! Never cross the street without an adult. Never! Do you hear me? Did you see that car? Never!" I could feel people watching. I was digging my fingers into your shoulders too deeply, and you cried because it hurt, but I didn't care. It was worth it. I just thought, *She has to remember this, this might be my chance to save her*.

I think about Kathy all the time.

I wonder if she lives for the mention of Aaron's name, hearing some story she'd forgotten or never knew, seeing his handwriting in a high school notebook under the sofa, an old photograph, a few frames of video. *Here he is at his christening, or holding out a handful of roly-poly bugs, or playing stickball in that field across from the Wawners' house. Remember how he brought a one-pound bag of M&M's to that girl he had a crush on—Carmen?—or how many times he snuck off to the lake to go fishing and then confessed—he could never lie—before going to sleep? Remember how he'd be lying back on his bed with his hands behind his head, looking at the ceiling, and when you'd ask him what he was doing, he'd say,* talkin' to God, *or how, when we lived on the farm, he was always climbing that tree and then jumping out, over and over, like he was practicing for a jumping-out-of-trees contest?*

I wonder if Kathy ever forgets entirely, then hates herself when it comes rushing back at her. I wonder whether she tells strangers that she has two kids or three. I wonder if she sometimes goes to sleep on a bed of Aaron's clothes, breathing them in like so many scent squares.

I asked her recently if she ever wanted to kill herself. I don't remember exactly how I put it, but she knew what I was getting at. She said no. She was still Maggie's Momma and Lena's Ma. She was still Tony's wife. Someone still needed to fill Satchel's dog bowl and take him for walks twice a day. There were still rivers to float on and yellow moons that stopped her short in the night and diner food. There were still days when she had the urge to wear her leopard-print loafers, something a seething person could not possibly do. There were still close lacrosse games that got her up on her feet and

Camp Wahoo, a place Aaron loved, where you could wear nothing but a bathing suit and flip-flops for days, play flashlight tag and paint rocks and build fires that lasted past midnight. There were still terrible arguments and painful conversations, confessions, makeup sex and speechless moments, and there were still sobbing children to be held and righted and sent back out into the world. All that wicked, wrenching aching could not nullify the fact that there was still a role for her—work to be done and happiness to be had.

She was sad, not bitter. "There's a difference," she said.

———

I remember having an awful conversation once, long before I became a mother, about whether it would be worse to lose a baby or a ten-year-old or a twenty-year-old, and so on. Why people think about these things, I don't know, but we do. We hover around the edges of catastrophe—trading headlines, reading memoirs about addiction and disease and abuse, watching seventeen seasons of *ER*. I said it would hurt the most to lose a twenty-year-old, because you'd have loved them so much longer and your attachment would be so much more specific. Babies love everyone and everyone loves them. But twenty-year-olds? They won't lean into just anyone. You have to earn any sliver of intimacy you share with them. Some pale memory of trust and connection has to hold against the callous disregard that is adolescence. And at twenty, they are just on their way back to you.

Now, though, for me, the most unthinkable loss would be never to have had a child in the first place. That's what I ended up saying to Meg (your "Aunt" Meg, who became family when we asked her to be Claire's godmother).

I don't know why Meg's single. She's crazy-accomplished—marathons, fund-raising projects with Tom Brokaw, conference calls with Bono. She almost went to ballet school instead of college and still has Dancer Ass. She has a master's from the Kennedy School and worked for the World Bank. She reads *The Economist* and *People*.

But that's not why I love her. I love her because she gave her friend most of her savings when the financial markets imploded—in fact, she insisted on it. I love her because she pinches mold off her bread instead of tossing the loaf, she bakes casseroles, and always sends thank-you notes, like the well-raised girl from Topeka that she is. I love her because she has photographs all over her apartment of African villagers from her Peace Corps years, but none of the frames match and they're hung willy-nilly and all the nails and wires show. I love the way she is with her sister and brothers, how they tease each other and roll their eyes and say *Duh* but keep coming back together—helping with cable modems, flat tires, moves. I love that they are going to puke when they read this nice stuff about Meg and start calling her something totally juvenile like Mold Pincher.

I meet people at cocktail parties all the time, women who are moody or mean-spirited, and then their charming husband comes up with a nice, fresh drink for them and I always think, what does she have that Meg doesn't? Why does this woman get someone to sleep next to, someone to call when the dryer breaks, someone to bitch about to her friends? Meg is so much better. I'd marry her in a second.

Sometimes, when I'm with you girls, I kind of shake my head and say Meg's name out loud, almost like a prayer, which means that I'm thinking about how unfazed she'd be by the Play-Doh in your teeth or how much she would like the fairy hut you built or the way you made yourself a math worksheet and then filled in all the answers and gave yourself a big A+. I want her to have this thing I have that's so ordinary and tedious and aggravating, and then, so divine.

It's no small thing to encourage someone to become a single parent, to take on the bottomless work and cost and heartache that comes with children. Dad thought I might not want to push it. He thought Meg would do fine with the logistics and frustrations, the "blocking and tackling," as he put it. He was more worried about the unknowns. What if she adopts and the parents show up later and want the kid back? What if her child turns out to have learning disabilities or a genetic disease, or deep, unresolvable anger? What if some future boyfriend walks away, saying he really loves her kid—but he wants to have "his own"?

That conversation slowed me a bit. But then, Dad's a man. And he was talking about regret. I just couldn't imagine it would come to that. Mothers never come to regret their children, right? Not the mother of the trisomy baby who is born with his intestines on the outside and only lives for weeks, not the mother of the schizophrenic on *America's Most Wanted*, not the mother of the fifty-six-year-old who lives at home and drinks in the morning— no mother regrets her child. Right?

The weekend Meg turned forty, we drove to Tomales Bay. On the ride up, we got talking about our first road trip, twelve years before, to Lake Tahoe.

"You know the first thing I liked about you?" I said. "You blush. I don't know anyone who blushes." She laughed. "I don't!" I said. "And I think it's so funny because you're such a competent person. I mean, you're not silly or girly or even remotely giddy. You know?"

"Yeah. Although . . . ," she said, glancing at a CD in her car door pocket.

"Yes, there is that. That has always troubled me." Meg is the only person I know who listens, unironically, to John Denver. She cried when they announced his plane had crashed. She also loved *Titanic*, a crap movie that got way too much credit. But other than those two flaws, which are probably linked by some kind of rogue gene, Meg is solid.

"You know what I liked about you?" Meg said. "You didn't hold anything back. You were right out there."

But I was holding something back. Partly because we are, all of us, always holding things back. And partly because I was nervous, afraid that as soon as I said what I wanted to say, she'd think I'd given up on her chances for marriage or, worse, that I'd never believed they were particularly good to begin with. "I have something I want to say." My voice cracked. "I want to say that as much as I love Edward and love being married—which I really do—there is no relationship that has been more—"

"I know where you're going," she said.

"Should I go there anyway?"

"Yes."

"So I know this isn't the way it's supposed to be and know I can't say what it'd be like to be a single mom . . . " We were both facing forward, looking at the road. "But given everything I do know, no matter how hard it is, how lonely or stressful, still, I would not want to leave this earth without being a mother."

She nodded.

"And you—I think you, in particular, were born to be somebody's mother."

She hit her blinker and switched lanes. I rode out the silence. I had said enough.

"I think," she said through tears, "I could be a

really good mom." We sat with that for a minute, and then she added, "I went to a sperm bank Web site."

"You did?"

"I did."

A few months later, Dad took over the morning routine so I could go with Meg to the fertility clinic for her procedure. It took fifteen minutes. When the nurse opened the door and Meg appeared, I wanted to scoop her up like a new bride so all that sperm from donor 11874 didn't fall out. On the ride home, we talked about what would happen if it worked.

"How will I tell my mom? My dad?" Meg asked. "My *grandmother*?"

"I don't know. I mean, you'll tell them that you really wanted to have children."

"They're not gonna like this."

"They love you," I said, meaning something entirely different than I'd ever meant before. I felt so sure, having become a parent myself, I could speak for them now. "They want you to be happy."

A week later, Meg got her period.

"Maybe this is the way it's supposed to be," she said on the phone, sounding like a mother already, prepared to sacrifice her own happiness for the sake of her child.

The choices we have are staggering. You girls will have even more.

In time, Meg tried again.

"It worked," she said when I picked up the phone.

Every hair on my arms lifted. "Really?"

"Really."

I screamed and you both came running into my office and we turned to October 2 in my calendar. I colored in the entire day, line by line, with my orange highlighter. When you saw the tears coming down my cheeks, you said, "What's so wrong about October second?" and I said, "Not wrong. October second is the day Meg becomes a mom."

I studied you girls that afternoon, like art. Your collarbones, your coloring, your shoulder blades—fine and slender as a bird's. Claire, you were sitting by the French doors to the deck that needs replacing, wearing only your underwear and the ruby red slippers Meg gave you that were years away from fitting. As you leaned forward to run your finger over the sequins, the light hit the trail of hair that swirls down from your hairline in the back and it lit up like phosphorescence. Georgia, you were up in the bath with your eyes closed and your ears just under the water, your hair spread out around your face, humming that song from *Les Miserables* that you saw Susan Boyle sing on YouTube.

Who will look at you like I do?

I think about your futures a lot. I often want to whisper to you, when we're tangled up together or I'm pinning your poetry to the bulletin board or repositioning the pillow under your head so you don't get a crick, *Remember this. This is what love feels like. Don't take less.* But what I end up saying is, "This was my dream. You were my dream." I've said it too many times though; now when I look at you all soft and gushy and say, "Guess what?" you say, "This was your dream. I was your dream."

A month later, Meg was still pregnant.

"I'm going to go see my grandmother. She's not

gonna live for nine more months. I gotta tell her," Meg said.

We practiced over the phone as she drove down to the airport. I thought the key was to lead her grandmother there so that she'd know what Meg was going to say before she said it.

"So I'll start by talking about how I always wanted to be a mom."

"Right, perfect."

"Okay." She sounded resolute but then she came back with, "She got married when she was nineteen."

"And?"

"She's one of the most conservative people I know, Kelly. She goes to church every day. The church that won't give condoms to Africans with AIDS. What do you think they think about babies out of wedlock? From online sperm banks?"

In St. Louis, Meg sat in the living room with her grandmother and told her.

"Oh thank *God*," said the woman born in 1912.

Meg looked up.

"I always worried that your brains and beauty were gonna go to waste. Go in my bedroom. There's some knitting by the window. Yellow."

On the radiator, Meg found a tiny sweater, almost complete. The buttons were pinned on and the second sleeve still needed to be attached.

"I wasn't sure who I was knitting that for," her grandmother called out from the other room. "Isn't that something? I just was knitting a baby sweater for no one in particular. And now I know. Isn't that something?"

So girls, will you please believe me when I tell

you that I love you enough to take in the full reality of your lives? That I can understand the things you think I can't and I can see and know and embrace every bit of you, full frame, no cropping?

———

This morning, Georgia, you slipped into bed with me before six. After some adjusting and resettling, you said, "You know what I've noticed?"

"What?" I asked.

"A lot of times, elbows are bent."

"It's true."

"That's why the skin is so wrinkly on the tips," you said, finding my elbow under the sheets as Claire appeared in the doorway looking like a cross between Sandy Duncan and Jeff Spicoli.

"I know some people who never bend their elbows," she said.

"Who?" you demanded.

"The people in the straightest-arm-club," Claire said, in her singsong voice.

"There's no such thing!"

"Yes there is."

"Where?" you said.

"In Arkansas," Claire said.

"Mom, tell her!" you said, a tireless champion for Truth against nonsense.

"Oh boy," I said, looking in the direction of the clock without my glasses. "Does that say seven?"

After breakfast, I sent you both upstairs to brush your teeth, something that never seems to take long enough, while I cleaned up the kitchen; the last few bloated Cheerios, a nearly finished lanyard you started at Camp Tockwogh, a cootie catcher we'd made that predicted the future—*You will be on* American Idol, *You will swim in the Olympics, You will live in Bora Bora*—a third-grade spelling list that started with *enough* and ended with *ground,* a homemade book that said: *Once upon a time*—blank page, blank page—*The End.* I put that in a drawer. Maybe I'll throw it out later, maybe not—I never know which souvenirs to keep.

We walked to the bus stop.

You guys wanted me to let you wait alone. You told me to "stop babying you," so I stood 143 steps away.

I could still see you. But God, you were small on that corner. If I'd taken a picture, you'd have been just two shapes.

The bus pulled up, the doors opened, kids called out your names. You were fine—better than fine. I was there. I saw it.

DEDICATION

My mother recently found a snapshot of Aaron and asked Kathy if she should send the photo down to Charlottesville. "I have enough photos of him," Kathy said. "You keep it. Put it on your bulletin board and when someone asks who he is, tell them about Aaron, everything you know. Tell them he loved taking things apart to see how they worked and that, if the weather allowed, he pretty much had to be outside. Tell them that he was a joker and an optimist and a ponderer of great and small things. Tell them that he loved horseshoes, paint guns and slingshots, Donut Sticks, Steak-umms, four-wheeling and camping and Led Zeppelin. Tell them if he loved you, you'd never forget how good it felt."

This book is for Kathy, in memory of her son, Aaron Corrigan Zentgraf, a boy you would've been lucky to know. Love you, Kath.

AARON

GEORGIA

CLAIRE

MEG'S BABY

Meg and her daughter live in San Francisco and are thriving. However, if you know a guy, a special and good man (preferably born before 1970), I trust you'll let me know.